Spirit FILLED'

JACK HAYFORD

Foursquare Media

1910 W. Sunset Blvd.
Los Angeles, California 90026
www.foursquaremedia.org

All Bible quotations are taken from The Living
Bible, copyright 1971 by Tyndale House
Publishers Wheaton, Illinois, unless indicated as
being from The Holy Bible, New King James
Version (NKJV), Copyright 1979, 1980, 1982 by
Thomas Nelson, Inc., Nashville, Tennessee.

Foursquare Media
1910 W. Sunset Blvd.
Los Angeles, CA 90026
www.foursquaremedia.org

ISBN 0-9635581-7-X
Copyright 1984 by Jack Hayford Ministries
Reprint 2007, Foursquare Media

Spirit FILLED

Jack W. Hayford

CONTENTS

INTRODUCTION

"Little children…you have an anointing
from the Holy One, and…the anointing
which you have received from Him abides
in you" (1 John 2:18-27 NKJV).

To be Spirit-filled is to come to the King
Himself—to bow at Jesus' feet and receive divine
power from His own hand.

The be Spirit-filled is to have the Holy
Spirit—the "oil of heaven"—poured from God's
throne into your own being; to be anointed by
Christ the King.

There are *three reasons* Jesus Christ wants to
anoint every redeemed son and daughter of God,
three abilities He wants to enhance and expand in
each of us, and *three offices* He wants to fulfill.

He wants to anoint us for these three reasons:

1. However sincere we may be, we cannot,
   on our own, *worship* God as freely and
   fully as He deserves.
2. However zealous we may be, we cannot,
   on our own, *witness* for Christ as effec-
   tively as He desires.
3. However zealous we may be, we cannot,
   on our own, do *warfare* for Christ as pene-
   tratingly as He directs.

The three abilities Christ wants to give us through the Holy Spirit are these:

1. An *expansion* of our capacity for worshiping
2. An *extension* of our dynamic for witnessing
3. An *expulsion* of the Adversary through our spiritual warfare

Then there are three *offices* that involve our receiving an anointing:

1. Priests
2. Prophets
3. Kings

At the heart of this marvelous plan, arranged by the Lord Jesus Christ to ensure our sufficiency for true Christian living, is a beautiful Old Testament picture: the practice of anointing— of pouring holy oil upon candidates for the holy offices of priest, prophet, and king. This anointing was a symbol of the Holy Spirit of God being poured on them to energize and bless them for their tasks.

Each of these offices or positions presents an example from which we can learn and a role that we are to fulfill. The Spirit-filled life of expanded worship (as priests), extended witness (as prophets), and expelling warfare (as kings) is no accidental parallel. The Holy Spirit is given to us so that we may experience all God foresaw and designed from the beginning.

"In the last days," God said, "I will pour out my Holy Spirit upon all mankind" (Acts 2:17).

Thus, as New Testament priests, we are *elevated* to allow us to offer new dimensions of sacrifice in our worship to God Almighty, Creator of us all.

"You have been chosen by God Himself —you are priests of the King, you are holy and pure, you are God's very own—all this so that you may show to others how God called you out of the darkness into His wonderful light" (1 Peter 2:9).

As New Testament prophets, we are *enabled* to reach new dimensions of worldwide witness in the Name of Jesus of Nazareth, the Son of God.

"But when the Holy Spirit has come upon you, you will receive power to testify about Me with great effect, to the people in Jerusalem, throughout Judea, in Samaria, and to the ends of the earth, about My death and resurrection" (Acts 1:8).

And as New Testament kings, we are *enriched* to rule with new dimensions of kingdom authority and power.

"To Him who loved us and washed us from our sins in His own blood, and has made us kings and priests to His God and Father" (Revelation 1:5, 6, NKJV).

The Spirit-filled life is the new-dimensional life of worship, witness, and warfare. And the key to its realization is the anointing Jesus places on your life—like heavenly oil poured over the heads of priests, prophets and kings in ancient times. And that anointing is the result of being filled with, overflowed by, and baptized in the Holy Spirit.

This promised anointing is for everyone who has received Jesus as their Savior. So let us take hold of the new dimensions of practical spirituality available in that anointing by coming to Christ and allowing Him to release His Spirit in us all!

Spirit-filled!
Let nothing but your light
shine through me, Lord.

Spirit-filled!
Now penetrate me
with Your Spirit's Sword.

Spirit-filled!
Come Jesus, now
according to your Word.

Spirit-filled!
Your promise shall no longer
be ignored.

Spirit-filled!
As those at Pentecost
in one accord.

Spirit-filled!
Dear Jesus, give me
what I can't afford.

Spirit-filled!
Your free gift now upon me b
e outpoured.

Spirit-filled!
O Jesus, with these lips
now be adored.

CHAPTER ONE

The Promise and The Patterns

IMAGINE YOUR HEART filled with God's love, your mind filled with God's truth, your soul filled with God's life, and your body overflowing with God's goodness. That's what the promise of "being filled with the Holy Spirit" opens to us—the invitation to be filled with God.

Anyone who has tasted the love of God in Jesus Christ, who has been forgiven of sin and been newborn into the family of God, has already found that the Lord is good. Now Christ calls us to *be filled* with that goodness.

Becoming "Spirit-filled" is the third step in obeying God's call to each of us. Those three steps are outlined in the famous sermon the Apostle Peter preached on Pentecost—the day the Church was born. The phenomenal happenings of that day are recorded in specific detail in the Book of Acts, chapter 2. God's Word is careful to show us how He wants the Church to be, so the foundational patterns found in Acts are important to our study.

Basic to our understanding is what occurred as Peter preached. People began to ask, "What should we do?" Their questions were provoked by what they had seen, heard, and understood of Peter's message and the events preceding it. Basically, this is what had happened:

1. Jesus left His disciples, commanding them to wait in Jerusalem until the Holy Spirit was given. They prayerfully obeyed.

2. On the Day of Pentecost (the day celebrating the Jewish beginning of harvest), the power of God's Spirit came with dramatic, stirring signs.

3. Jesus' disciples were "filled with the Holy Spirit" and miraculously began speaking languages they hadn't learned, as Jesus had prophesied (Mark 16:17).

4. Attracted and puzzled by this miracle of language, many attending the feast-day celebration asked, "What can this mean?" Peter rose to answer, explaining that the whole occasion was a fulfillment of God's promise to fill all who love and serve Him with His Holy Spirit.

5. In explaining this miracle, Peter went on to proclaim Jesus Christ as Savior and King. He emphasized that many of those who heard Christ in person were guilty of joining in His crucifixion, and that, since His resurrection now *proved* Jesus to be the Son of God, they stood guilty of a terrible deed before God Himself.

6. Thousands were deeply moved as they faced this truth that was so miraculously verified in their midst. The testimony of Jesus' resurrection was being mightily affirmed, both by the message Peter preached and by the miracle of

speech they still heard as the believers continued lifting praise to God for His glorious works.

7. With that, many cried aloud: "What should we do?" Peter's answer outlined the three steps every seeker must take to enter into a growing walk with Jesus:

"Each one of you must turn from sin, return to God, and be baptized in the Name of Jesus Christ for forgiveness of your sins; then you also shall receive this gift, the Holy Spirit. For Christ promised Him to each one of you who has been called by the Lord our God, and to your children and even to those in distant lands!" (Acts 2:38, 39).

Here then, from Peter's statement at Pentecost, are the three steps to which God calls everyone who will answer His call and walk in His ways:

First, repent! Turning from sin to the Savior is the pathway of new birth. All who obey this step are *newborn* (John 3:3).

Second, be baptized! Water baptism is a command of Jesus Christ (Matthew 28:18, 19), and all who obey declare Him as their Lord.

Third, receive the Holy Spirit! This promised gift has been available to each one of us since that day, as surely as the gift of forgiveness and the call to be baptized are available.

It is important for us to see this simple fact

---

as clearly as it is emphasized in the Bible. It is as though Peter anticipated that future generations would wonder if the same blessing, benefit, and promise received by the Church at its birth would still be available as time and distance changed. He not only stresses to those hearing him *that* day, but asserts that the same things would always be available, regardless of time.

> "For the promise is to you and to your children, and to all who are afar off, as many as the Lord our God will call" (Acts 2:39, NKJV).

"To all who are afar off" is a beautifully inclusive phrase. It covers all *races* (The Gentile world would be included too, in time.), all *geographic locations* (The whole world would be reached with time.), and all *generations* (Though centuries would pass, the promise was made available to all people in all places at all times!).

This booklet is about being Spirit-filled in the same way and for the same purpose as those earliest disciples were filled—and by the same Holy Spirit.

But this booklet is about more than being Spirit-filled; it is about *you* being Spirit-filled. "This promise is for you!"

What a promise! *You* can be filled with God's Spirit just as Jesus intends all of His servants to be. Capturing a sense of how fully available that promise is always fills earnest hearts with a passion to be filled. So let the promise of God whet your appetite. Now that you've tasted the Lord in repentance and salvation and found Him good—and since His Holy Spirit already *dwells* in you as one of His redeemed children—discover how He can *fill and overflow* your life.

The Holy Spirit—who gives inner witness that Jesus is now your Savior and that you are God's child—wants you to take your next step and let Jesus overflowingly fill you with His life, love, and power. What Christ has introduced *by* His Spirit, He is ready to expand *with* His Spirit. The promise of Pentecost is yours to be received from Jesus' own hand. The Holy Spirit is "given by God to those who obey Him" (Acts 5:32).

CHAPTER TWO

The Promise and The Passion

THERE IS SOMETHING of an urgency in the Scriptures surrounding the matter of being Spirit-filled. Even Jesus is urgent about it.

1. The night before He was crucified, Jesus spent a great deal of time teaching His disciples of the "Comforter" (Helper) who would come—the Holy Spirit (John 14:16).

2. Following His resurrection, Christ urged His disciples to prepare their hearts to receive the Holy Spirit (John 20:21, 22).

3. And, just before He ascended to heaven, Christ made three pointed statements about His disciples being filled with the Holy Spirit:

   a. *Its certainty*: "You shall." In one of these meetings He told them not to leave Jerusalem until the Holy Spirit came upon them in fulfillment of the Father's promise, a matter He had previously discussed with them. "John baptized you with water," He reminded them, "but you shall be baptized with the Holy Spirit in just a few days" (Acts 1:4, 5).

   b. *Its priority*: "Stay here until." "And now I will send the Holy Spirit upon you, just as My Father promised. Don't begin telling others yet—stay here in the city until the Holy Spirit comes and fills you with power from heaven" (Luke 24:49).

c. *Its ability*: "Receive power." "But when the Holy Spirit has come upon you, you will receive power to testify about Me with great effect, to the people in Jerusalem, throughout Judea, in Samaria, and to the ends of the earth, about My death and resurrection" (Acts 1:8).

Jesus' several references to the need for His disciples to be Spirit-filled make clear His concern that no one neglect this third step of obedience. He wants to take us past the human tendency to be comfortable with as little effort as possible. Since forgiveness of sins ensures us of eternal life in heaven, and since water baptism indicates our willingness to become disciples under His authority and Lordship, we might be inclined to simply stop there.

But the Spirit-filled life Christ calls us to is one of divine fullness and powerful ability to spread the love of God. He wants us to receive His power and then touch the world around us as we can do only when we have the might of His Spirit in us: "Not by might, nor by power, but by My Spirit, says the Lord of Hosts" Zechariah 4:6). This is a heavenly reminder that our best cannot begin to equal God's almightiness!

Jesus' passionate concern that His disciples be filled with the Holy Spirit was also seen in the early Church leaders at two notable times:

1. *Samaria, A.D. 36.* Acts 8 gives us the remarkable report of a sweeping revival that hit the city of Samaria about six years after Pentecost. Philip's mighty evangelistic ministry had led many to Christ—great deliverances had occurred, and he had led many to water baptism.

But when Peter and John arrived from Jerusalem to observe the situation in Samaria, they indicated their concern that none of the converts had yet been filled with the Holy Spirit, "for as yet He had not come upon any of them, for they had only been baptized in the Name of the Lord Jesus" (Acts 8:16).

Peter and John were quick to extend that ministry to the new believers, recognizing the importance of this third step. The Bible is clear that these believers of Samaria had believed and had been baptized in water (v.12). Now, to move them along to deeper discipleship, Peter and John prayed for them and laid hands on them. When they did these things, the Bible says the new believers "received the Holy Spirit" (vv. 15-17).

Furthermore, their experience was neither a mere formality nor a casual exercise. Something so significant occurred when they received the Holy Spirit that Simon, the sorcerer, wanted to buy this power from the apostles (v. 18). As at Pentecost when the first believers were filled with the Holy Spirit, it was evident that something had happened!

Any notion that such a *filling* experience

---

would be less than unusual should be laid aside. When He fills us with the Holy Spirit, Jesus Christ is doing something special, and we can welcome that prospect with peaceful confidence in the light of and with faith in the Word of God.

2. *Ephesus, A.D. 49.* Acts 19 reports a similar situation. Paul went to Ephesus and encountered disciples who, though believers, were not fully advised about Jesus. Recognizing that—though they had been baptized in water—something was still missing, he asked them, "Did you receive the Holy Spirit when you believed?" (v.2). They answered that they had never even heard of that possibility. Though they clearly and truly loved God, they had been baptized in obedience to John the Baptist's teaching about repentance, not fully aware of who Jesus was…and is. Paul called them to a full belief in Jesus and to be baptized again in the Name of the Lord Jesus. As they responded, Paul laid his hands upon their heads—and "the Holy Spirit came on them, and they spoke in other languages and prophesied" (v.6). It was a revisitation of Pentecost!

It is worthy to note the passion that occupied the minds of early Church leaders: They knew every disciple needed to be Spirit-filled. The actions of Peter, John and Paul verify two things: (1) It was unsatisfactory for disciples to stop short of Holy Spirit-fullness; and (2) when people received the Holy Spirit, there was clear evidence of the Spirit at work. They did not consider this experience either optional or mystical. Jesus had commanded it, so it wasn't to be taken casually. And the work of the Spirit was mightily evident; there was no mysticism or guesswork about it. God was present, working purely and powerfully in believers who were newly Spirit-filled.

In each scriptural account of believers who received the promised Holy Spirit, we see the reality of God's work in their lives. This is why Jesus still calls us to be filled with the Holy Spirit. Having heard this call, and having seen the biblical evidence of the fulfillment of this promise, let's study the *purpose* for being Spirit-filled.

CHAPTER THREE

The Purpose of The Promise

WHEN WE DISCUSS CHRIST'S PURPOSE in our being filled with the Spirit, we are not discussing a passing moment of blessing or an experience to be realized and then shelved.

Entering into the fullness of the Holy Spirit is exactly that—an *entrance*. It is the point at which Jesus intends for us to enter a partnership with Him; a partnership of extending and ministering His life, His love, and His power to others.

This is dramatically illustrated in Jesus' words: "For the Scriptures declare that rivers of living water shall flow from the inmost being of anyone who believes in Me" (John 7:38).

His emphasis is on our *outward flow*—streams of life-giving water overflowing the inner man and refreshing others. The force of this "river" image is multiplied when held in contrast with an earlier figure of speech.

In John 4, Jesus talked with a very needy woman. He saw her sin as the action of a longing, thirsty soul seeking satisfaction. So, in confronting her, He addressed her spiritual *thirst*. As He did so, He gave His answer to every deep, human quest for lasting fulfillment:

"Whoever drinks of the water that I shall give him will never thirst. But the water that I shall give him will become in him a fountain of water springing up unto everlasting life" (John 4:14, NKJV).

His graphic word picture depicts an inner well, a fountain to satisfy each person's thirst. But then, as we read in John 7, the well overflows to form "rivers" that serve the thirst of others.

The *first* is immediate, personal, and internal; the *second* is expansive, out-flowing, and extending.

The first is that thirst-satisfying provision of Christ as the Water of life, satisfying our sin-parched souls; the second is the Holy Spirit, coming like mighty streams of power flowing from God, surging from within the believer and carrying the refreshing life of God to others in need.

The first figure is Jesus' gift of life to me and in me, answering my need; the second is the Holy Spirit's power through me and from me, channeling Christ's life to answer the human needs around me.

The strategy was plain: Jesus Christ planned to fill all of His followers with so much of His life and love that their overflow would extend His power to others. John explains conclusively that the "rivers" were to come after Pentecost:

"He was speaking of the Holy Spirit, who would be given to everyone believing in Him; but the Spirit had not yet been

given, because Jesus had not yet returned
to His glory in heaven" (John 7:39).

So today, all we who believe have a well of
life within us to answer our own thirst. And to
fulfill Christ's highest purposes, He promises
that His Holy Spirit will stream through us and
beyond us—to the world.

THE MOST IMPORTANT REASON

There are several scriptural and practical reasons
that every believer in Jesus Christ needs to be
Spirit-filled, but towering above them all is this
one: The power of the Holy Spirit is the power
by which Jesus carried out His entire ministry.

When Jesus went to John for baptism, He said
that His baptism was essential: "For I must do all
that is right" (Matthew 3:15). Immediately, the
Holy Spirit descended upon Him and His preparation for ministry was complete.

We might well ask, "Why did Jesus need
special preparation for ministry? After all, He was
God!" And, of course, that is true. Yet, when He
went to John for baptism Christ said, "This is
essential to fulfill all righteousness" (Matthew
3:15 NKJV). Since He was sinless, the "righteousness" to which Jesus referred is clearly not an
act of repentance. What He referred to is what
occurred when He was baptized: the Holy Spirit
came upon Him!

This is a simple but demanding point to be

---

understood. Jesus Himself, though born of the Holy Spirit as the sinless and perfect Son of God (Luke 1:35), still needed another dimension of power for His ministry. This is not to minimize Christ's person, as though He were less than God. Rather it emphasizes how truly He became a man. Philippians 2:1-10 describes how Christ voluntarily surrendered His divine powers as God so that He could live and serve the Father's will on completely human terms. In short, His perfection and purity were not of themselves sufficient for the task He faced. As God He was completely holy, but as a man He was completely helpless to accomplish His ministry. Unless...unless, as a man, He could draw upon the full resources of heaven's power.

The remarkable thing about this is how dramatically it reveals God's plan for restoring fallen mankind. Jesus is shown at His baptism to be the Father's provision for recovering humankind's double loss. (Through sin, Adam lost not only his open relationship with God but also his God-given rulership in life.) Thus, through Jesus' sinlessness, God revealed His Son as the way for man to restore his relationship with God: "This is my beloved Son, and I am wonderfully pleased with him" (Matthew 3:17). Then, in the descent of the Holy Spirit upon Jesus, God unfolded His plan for allowing man to recover rulership as well: "The heavens were opened to Him and He saw the Spirit of God coming down in the form of a dove" (Matthew 3:16).

Spirit Filled

Thus, in Christ, we have been given a dual resource: (1) The *presence* of the Holy Spirit within, affirming that we are acceptable to God and assisting our growing relationship with Him; and (2) the *power* of the Holy Spirit filling and overflowing us, developing God's kingdom authority in our lives and extending that rule of love through us to others.

Here then is His double gift: relationship and rulership—being able to know Him and to make Him known. At Christ's baptism, the fulfillment of "all that is right" became a possibility available to us because of the way Jesus fulfilled His ministry.

GRASPING THE IMPLICATIONS

There is a joy-inspiring reality in all of this: The Lord Jesus wants to place within each one of us exactly the same power and ability that He had for ministry.

If Christ had fulfilled His ministry simply by the sheer power at His disposal as Second Person of the Godhead, it would, of course, have been wonderful to behold. But for us—we ordinary humans—there would remain one awkward reality. When He would in turn call us to serve Him with dedication as disciples and with power to impact a world of need, He would be asking us to do something never before done on this planet. There would be no prototypes or examples. We could review Jesus' life and ministry, but that wouldn't be quite the same, for He would have accomplished His mission by His power "as God," without knowing or experiencing human limitations.

But the Bible tells us that He chose another pathway:

> "Jesus Christ, though He was God, did not demand and cling to His rights as God, but laid aside His mighty power and glory, taking the disguise of a slave and becoming like men" (Philippians 2:6,7).

The heart of an incredible truth lies in the words, "He laid aside His mighty power and glory." This literally means Jesus emptied Himself of all His inherent powers as God. *All of His life was lived on human terms*, but carried out by the divine power He drew on daily, just as He calls us to do. Although He lived His human life just as any other human being, of course there was one dramatic difference: He never sinned. Because He was born of God, sin was never in Him and He never surrendered to it.

But Jesus came to do even more than to live sinlessly and die as our sinless sacrifice. In doing that, He has become our Savior, but His goal was not just to save sinners. He also came to break the curse and to become Lord of a new breed of men—a redeemed race. Besides living perfectly and dying to pay the penalty of death for mankind's sin, He also came to destroy all the works of the Devil and regain the authority mankind lost. His Cross does both: restores our relationship with God and breaks hell's dominion on earth. Jesus has begotten a new "body" of people: the Church—the redeemed sons and daughters of God. And He wants to fill each of us with the power that will enable us to do what He did, to advance His mission of life, love, health, and wholeness for all mankind.

> "For this purpose the Son of God was manifested, that He might destroy the works of the devil…You are of God, little children, and have overcome them, because He who is in you is greater than He who is in the world…For whatever is born of God overcomes the world" (1 John 3:8; 4:4; 5:4 NKJV).

Jesus' mission to begin a new race as well as to recover a lost one required a breakthrough in humanity's possibilities—not only making forgiveness possible, but evidencing the potential of man's triumph in life. By fulfilling His ministry as a man, daily drawing upon the Holy Spirit's power rather than utilizing His own special, personal powers as God, He presents us with conclusive evidence: victorious service to God is possible for redeemed Spirit-filled human beings. Christ has paved the way. He brings us first unto new life and then into new dominion. He provides His redeemed with the same power He depended upon and used in introducing God's love, mercy and healing to mankind, and in over-throwing hell's strongholds.

The comparative chart summarizes it.

JESUS	HIS REDEEMED
He was born of the Holy Spirit (*Matthew 1:20; Luke 1:35*).	We are reborn by the Holy Spirit (*John 3:3-8; Romans 8:11*).
He was sinlessly perfect (*Matthew 4:1-11; 2 Corinthians 5:21*).	We are declared forgiven in Christ (*Acts 13:38, 39; Romans 5:9; 8:1*).
He received the Holy Spirit's power for His ministry (*Matthew 3:16; John 3:34, 35*).	We are commanded to receive the Holy Spirit's power for service (*Luke 24:49; Acts 1:8*).
He triumphed over the enemy and delivered the needy (*Luke 4:18-21; Acts 10:38*).	We are commissioned to the same ministry and victory (*Matthew 28:18-20; Mark 16:15-20*).

It is clear that God's purpose in salvation is not only to prepare us for heaven, but to equip us for earth. God's present purpose is to display Christ's love, power, and wisdom to all creation

(See Ephesians 3:8-11.). And that purpose can be realized as believers receive the power of the Holy Spirit—the same power Jesus used to minister as a servant and conquer as a king!

So, in calling us to be Spirit-filled, Jesus Christ draws us into the realm of realizing God's fuller purpose:

1. He has given us eternal life, but for greater purposes than simply "being saved."
2. He will fill us with the Holy Spirit as a further step toward realizing His highest destiny for us.
3. By that means, He qualifies and commissions us to extend His life, love, and power in the same way and by the same power that He used to minister.

The greater purpose of our being Spirit-filled is to receive the promise God offers to all who will hear His heart; who recognize His desire for a people who will let Him be, in them, "Jesus Christ, the same yesterday, today, and forever" (Hebrews 13:8). When we are filled with His Spirit, the world can be changed by His grace and power.

CHAPTER FOUR

The Person in The Promise

TO BE SPIRIT-FILLED is not to enter some mysterious relationship with God. There isn't anything abstract about it. But it *is* important to underscore the difference between being filled with God's Holy Spirit and being filled with any other kind of spirit. Jesus emphasized this when He said:

> "You men who are fathers—if your boy asks for bread, do you give him a stone? If he asks for fish, do you give him a snake? If he asks for an egg, do you give him a scorpion? (Of course not!) And if even sinful persons like yourselves give children what they need, don't you realize that your heavenly Father will do at least as much, and give the Holy Spirit to those who ask for Him?" (Luke 11:1-13).

The clear promise of the Savior is that anyone who asks to be filled with the Holy Spirit isn't going to come up with something dry (stone), destructive (scorpion), or satanic (snake). There are so many bizarre and fanatical things around, not to mention occult and demonic activities, that the Holy Spirit must be seen in stark contrast. We must see Him for who He is, distinctly and beautifully different from those from the realm of darkness and confusion who go under the general heading of "spirits."

Let's consider then, the personality of the Holy Spirit. What is He *really* like?

THE HOLY SPIRIT IS JUST LIKE JESUS

We know this is true because Jesus Himself said so. To help His disciples prepare for His departure and the Holy Spirit's coming, He said:

> "I will ask the Father and He will give you another Comforter, and He will never leave you. He is the Holy Spirit, the Spirit who leads into all truth. The world at large cannot receive Him, for it isn't looking for Him and doesn't recognize Him. But you do, for He lives with you now and someday shall be in you" (John 14:16, 17).

Notice first that, in asserting the sameness between the Holy Spirit and Himself, Jesus says, "I will send another Comforter." In saying this, He affirms the obvious: He was here to "comfort" or help people. That aspect of Jesus' nature was already known, but now He promised "another Comforter." In other words, "He'll help you the same way I have."

Jesus further asserts the similarity between

Himself and the Holy Spirit as He says, "You do [know Him] for He lives with you." In short, the Holy Spirit was so fully present in Jesus' own life and ministry that He tells His disciples, "He's no stranger to you. You've seen Him working in Me. Now He's going to do the same thing in you."

Of course, it is no surprise that the Holy Spirit would be just like Jesus, for He is *God the Spirit*, just as Jesus is *God the Son*. The grandeur of God's being is beyond us. The Bible teaches that He is so rich in His own being that He has a three-ness (a Trinity). Human imagination is stretched to its limits in attempting to comprehend this. Yet if the universe, which in itself is seemingly infinite in splendor, is but one of His creations, we shouldn't be bewildered by the proposition that God's being transcends our full understanding. His person is multiple within its unity: He is the *one eternal God*, complete in the threefold expression as Father, Son, and Spirit.

Thus, when we open ourselves to be filled with the Holy Spirit, we are essentially opening to the fullness of God's love as shown by the Father; the fullness of Jesus' life as revealed by the Son; and the fullness of the Spirit's power as it is displayed in the Word.

To be Spirit-filled, then, is to open ourselves so that we can be filled with God. An old gospel hymn expressed it this way:

"Filled with God, yes, filled with God.
Pardoned and cleansed and filled with God.

Filled with God, yes, filled with God.
Emptied of self and filled with God."

THE HOLY SPIRIT IS OUR TEACHER

In the warmest sense of the word, the Holy Spirit's personal ministry within us is that of a teacher: a patient, understanding, faithful instructor and guide. When He introduced the forthcoming work of the Holy Spirit to His disciples, Jesus said:

> "But when the Father sends the Comforter instead of Me—and by the Comforter I mean the Holy Spirit—He will teach you much, as well as remind you of everything I myself have told you" (John 14:26).

As a teacher, the Holy Spirit provides help that is not so much an academic process as one of inward instruction. He teaches us what to do and say at important times. He helps us keep our life—our conduct and our standards—in accordance with what Jesus wants and what the Bible says.

Since He is the one who gave the Scriptures, the Holy Spirit will dwell in us and prompt or correct us in our thoughts and behavior. At times that we might be inclined to violate the Word of God through ignorance or forgetfulness, like a teacher saying, "Remember…" or "Do this" or "Don't do this," He will help those who will listen and learn. You may be faced with something you haven't even learned as yet, but He'll correct you before you fail. A good teacher will not sacrifice your future understanding by allowing you to violate rules at the present moment because you haven't advanced to the later stage of knowledge. In other words, the Holy Spirit will keep you on track—helping you become more like Jesus as you grow in God's Word and will.

That's what Jesus meant when He taught that the Holy Spirit would "guide you into all truth" (John 16:13). The Spirit helps us understand and keeps us consistent with the Father's heart and purpose. But this requires that we listen to His inner promptings. An honest heart that looks toward God with integrity is a treasure in His eyes. The Holy Spirit is a faithful teacher, but He is also easily grieved—if rebuffed continually, He will stop teaching or correcting. He only keeps teaching the Father's sons and daughters who are open and willing to learn.

And, like a good teacher, the Holy Spirit is faithful to prepare us for tests. If we heed His voice and obey His promptings, we can be ready for any trial or test. And we will not only pass the test, but we'll find victory afterward.

THE HOLY SPIRIT IS OUR HELPER

"But when the Helper comes...He will testify of Me. And you also will bear witness"(John 15:26, 27 NKJV).

The Holy Spirit gives help of two kinds—Assistance and Dynamism.

ASSISTANCE FROM THE SPIRIT

This is simply strength—in the inner man (See Ephesians 3:16.). The inner help of the Spirit lends stamina and stability to each of us, enabling us to be like a tree that is well rooted and able to withstand storms of adversity. The Greek word for "helper" is *parakletos*, which means "called beside." The idea is simply that of someone calling someone else to come and help him when he is facing a job too big for one person. Imagine moving a table alone. Now imagine having someone to help. The greater ease and efficiency of doing the task with two instead of one is obvious.

Likewise, Jesus sent the Holy Spirit to help the Church in the task of touching the world with God's love. It isn't that we are unable to serve or love or that we are disabled from serving or loving without the Holy Spirit. But with His help, an immeasurable, supernatural enablement is realized. He not only strengthens us within and stabilizes us to withstand stormy circumstances, but He moves through us in power, bearing witness to Jesus Christ.

BEING DYNAMIC IN THE SPIRIT

This can be understood in Jesus' words from John 15:26: "He (the Holy Spirit) shall testify of Me

and you also will bear witness" (NKJV). The role
of a witness is essentially to provide evidence for
the case. A witness attests to the truth of certain
facts that are questioned in court. This figure of
speech used in this verse—*witness*—is completely
contemporary. Jesus is still standing trial in the
courtroom of a hostile world. Questions constantly
face us: "What makes you think Jesus is God?"
"Why do you think He is *alive?*" "How can you say
He is the *only* Savior?" The Early Church faced
those questions with the verifying dynamic of the
Holy Spirit, and He is still prepared to bear witness to the truth of our testimony. When we bear
witness to Christ, the Holy Spirit will confirm our
testimony with signs that show Jesus is real.

The Book of Acts might well be called "the
acts of the Holy Spirit," rather than "the acts of
the apostles." It contains the record of the young
Church, throbbing with the powerful enabling of
the Holy Spirit as He fulfilled Jesus' prophecies:
"I will build My Church; and all the powers of
hell shall not prevail against it" (Matthew 16:18).
"And those who believe shall use My authority to
cast our demons...they will be able to place their
hands on the sick and heal them" (Mark 16:17,
18). The record shows that the Holy Spirit not
only came to help believers speak of Jesus, but His
power testified to the reality that "this Jesus you
crucified (is) the Lord, the Messiah!" (Acts 2:36).
The evidence was in: Christ's miraculous power,
which verified His Lordship during His ministry
(See John 3:2; 5:36.), was clearly still alive and

working in the Early Church. And He is ready to do the same today.

THE SPIRIT AND THE WORD

Of course, not everyone needs a miracle to verify the truth of Christ in him. Jesus acknowledged that some people believe simply because the written witness of the Scriptures witnesses with power (See John 5:36-47.). This isn't surprising either, since the Holy Spirit is the one who has given us God's Word (See 2 Peter 1:19-21.). No wonder God's Word is powerful and alive:

> "For whatever God says to us is full of living power; it is sharper than the sharpest dagger, cutting swift and deep into our innermost thoughts and desires with all their parts, exposing us for what we really are" (Hebrews 4:12).

Yet, as powerful as His Word is, at times God has used signs and wonders for its verification—unusual evidences testifying that Jesus is alive indeed. The Holy Spirit's power still works today, proving that Jesus has not changed, that He is the same today in every dimension of His ministry as He was during His lifetime, and in the days of the Early Church as seen in the Book of Acts.

THE HOLY SPIRIT IS A CONVINCER

Jesus said, "It is best for you that I go away, for if I don't, the Comforter won't come. If I do, He will—for I will send Him to you. And when He has come He will convince the world of its sin, and of the availability of God's goodness and of deliverance from judgment. The world's sin is unbelief in Me; there is righteousness available because I go to the Father you shall see Me no more; there is deliverance from judgment because the prince of this world has already been judged" (John 16:7-11).

It is in this ministry of the Holy Spirit that something of the awareness of His being God breaks through. That He attests to the Word of God and to the fact of Jesus' power is all very good. But the convincing work He does is the heart of His dynamic ministry. He forces a decision. No one can remain passive when the Holy Spirit is at work. He convinces people that sin separates them from God; that Jesus is God, and that He is the focal point of salvation; and that this world system, engineered by Satan, is headed toward destruction. The Holy Spirit probes the hearts of people wherever believers invite His powerful working. He does what we could never do: He convinces people that God is right, that man needs a Savior, that Jesus is that Savior, and that eternal consequences are at stake. To more fully understand this work of the Spirit, we should notice two things:

1.   *He is the one who convicts and convinces.*
This is obvious in Jesus' words, but, amazingly
enough, a terrible human tendency exists even in
the most sincere believer to try and do this work
for the Holy Spirit. Sometimes zealous Christians
are so pushy in witnessing that they contradict
the love and graciousness of the Savior. Jesus was
never feisty or pushy when He was reaching out
to the lost or the needy. It is one thing to feel
compassion and another thing to be pushy.
Confidence in the Holy Spirit's ministry will help
keep that balance.

Let's learn to do with the Holy Spirit what
the widely advertised bus company asks its clients
to do: "Leave the driving to us." If we try to
"drive" too hard, we might easily drive people
away. But if we simply and faithfully speak of
Jesus' love, allowing the Holy Spirit's power to
minister through us, He will take over and bring
those we are talking with to Christ.

2.   *He convicts and convinces individuals.* Jesus'
promise that the Holy Spirit would convince the
world of sin, of righteousness, and of judgment is
not fulfilled on a "generic" basis. It doesn't happen all at once or to everyone at once. We all
know many people who couldn't care less about
Christ—some who blaspheme His Name and others who mock or ignore God's Word, often with a
seeming immunity. There appears to be no lack of
such people, and we who seek to witness often
wonder: "Is it doing any good at all?" But don't let
these people discourage you or cause you to

doubt. The Holy Spirit is fully capable of breaking through *all* hardness, indifference, or doubt. Sensitive witnessing is the sowing of seed, and with watering it will inevitably spring forth as growing plants do through concrete. Prayer is the way to water the seeds of witnessing; prayer introduces the cultivation of the Holy Spirit's ministry in such situations.

An early example of this "breakthrough" quality of the Holy Spirit's working is recorded in Acts 4. Peter and John were bitterly resisted by the officials in Jerusalem, pointedly told that they were not to speak of Jesus any more, then thrown in jail. The Bible describes their response:

"As soon as they were freed, Peter and John found the other disciples and told them what the Council had said. Then all the believers united in this prayer: "O Lord, Creator of heaven and earth and of the sea and everything in them—You spoke long ago by the Holy Spirit through our ancestor King David, Your servant, saying, 'Why do the heathen rage against the Lord, and the foolish nations plan their little plots against Almighty God" The kings of the earth unite to fight against Him and against the anointed Son of God!'

"That is what is happening here in this city today! For Herod the king, and

Pontius Pilate the governor, and all the Romans—as well as the people of Israel—are united against Jesus, Your anointed Son, Your holy servant. They won't stop at anything that You in Your wise power will let them do. And now, O Lord, hear their threats, and grant to Your servants great boldness in their preaching and send Your healing power, and may miracles and wonders be done by the Name of Your holy servant Jesus." After this prayer, the building where they were meeting shook and they were all filled with the Holy Spirit and boldly preached God's message" Acts 4:23-31.

Notice how the Holy Spirit came upon them with power. And see how the message of Christ went forth with new force.

When the witness of Jesus is rejected or resisted, the believer's pathway of power is prayer. The ensuing chapters of Acts report an ongoing cycle of surgings by the Holy Spirit. He moves upon people of every station in life and brings hosts of them to the Lord Jesus. And that same Holy Spirit is still able to bring people to the Lord today. Our role is not to attempt to convict others by zeal, arguments, or ability—that's His work. Our work is to bear witness to them of Jesus Christ, then pray for them, and let the Holy Spirit take over from there!

THE HOLY SPIRIT IS A GLORIFIER

There is something especially beautiful about the Holy Spirit's commitment to exalt Jesus. In announcing the Spirit's coming, Jesus said, "He shall praise Me and bring Me great honor by showing you My glory. All the Father's glory is mine; this is what I mean when I say that He will show you My glory" (John 16:14, 15).

The greatest evidence of the Holy Spirit's presence is this: If the Holy Spirit is at work, then Jesus will be praised; Jesus will be honored; Jesus will be worshiped as God's Son; and Jesus will be announced as Lord and King!

The Holy Spirit fills people's lives and makes Jesus real to them. The result is this praise, worship, honor, and exaltation of Jesus. As Jesus said, "He shall praise Me and bring Me great honor by showing you My glory." The Holy Spirit shows us that Jesus is more than a doctrine or a memory; the Spirit draws our hearts into Jesus' presence to capture an ever-deepening sense of who He is and how wonderful He is.

There is one absolute test of whether an experience is of God. If there is a genuine commitment to honor, to obey, to praise, and to worship and glorify the Lord Jesus, then the Holy Spirit is truly present. One thing is certain: Satan is not going to glorify the Son of God. And as for the flesh, it will inevitably find a way to glorify itself. So expect the Holy Spirit to work in your life by bringing you into new dimensions of loving, serving, worshiping, honoring, and glorifying the Lord Jesus Christ! And when you are looking for a place to assemble and fellowship with the people of the Lord, the hallmark of spiritual health (in a church) is that the Lord Jesus Christ is praised and worshiped. In such a place, the Holy Spirit will always be given the opportunity to work, the Word of God will regularly be taught, and the glory of the Lord will be in evidence.

The Holy Spirit's ministry of making Jesus real—glorifying Him—is His highest desire. And when His purposes are fulfilled in this facet of His ministry, you will welcome the Lord Jesus Christ's fullest working in your heart, and you will want to worship and adore Him all the more.

CHAPTER FIVE

Partaking of The Promise

IT WAS A SUNDAY MORNING during my senior year of high school. As on any Sunday, I was attending my home church—a strong, evangelical church in Oakland, California. The message of the morning, brought by a visiting speaker, was on the need we all have for increased spiritual power and Jesus' promised blessing of "power from on high."

The speaker concluded his message by calling for every believer to "be filled with the Holy Spirit," and then asked us all to bow in prayer.

The crucial moment had come. Up to that point I had listened with an open heart. But now I was faced with a specific decision: "Do you want to receive the fullness of the Holy Spirit?"

Suddenly the most peculiar combination of feelings gripped me. I felt both a deep hunger for God *and* an inexplicable, nagging fear of responding to that hunger. Why was it that I should feel such a love for Christ and such a desire to do His will, yet at the same time feel as though a dragline were attached to my soul?

It would be years before I would come to understand the reason for that hesitation. But now, after teaching and preaching for decades and seeing thousands come into the fullness of God's

Holy Spirit, I clearly realize how much Satan hates to see people filled with the Holy Spirit. He fears the fact that every believer who is filled with the life and energy that made Jesus' ministry so effective threatens his dark rule on this planet and overthrows his plans for destroying eternal souls. And so, when any child of God begins to hunger for more of the power of God, the Liar often comes to subtly and stealthily discourage, create doubt and somehow attempt to chill the soul with indefinable fears.

But that Sunday morning, in spite of my fears, I responded to the invitation. Making my way to the prayer room, I knelt down in simple openness to the Lord Jesus Christ, who had become my Savior six years earlier. And it was there, without pomp but with very clear understanding and a real sense of encounter, that I received the fullness of the Holy Spirit.

Now, in addressing you through these pages, we have come to the same place, to the point where we have talked enough *about* the promise of the Holy Spirit. Now, dear reader, the invitation is yours to partake of the promise yourself.

The desirability of being Spirit-filled is so very clear. I am sure you must feel it already. Furthermore, it is perfectly appropriate and timely that you *now* come to Jesus and ask the One who fills with the Holy Spirit, to fill you. Consider:

1. *Jesus commands you to be filled.* "Receive the Holy Spirit," Jesus says, "until (you are filled) with power from heaven, and you will receive

power to testify about Me with great effect" (John 20:22; Luke 24:49; Acts 1:8). Why would Jesus need to "command" us to receive a gift? The answer seems obvious: He knew fear would try to create questions and hesitancy, so His command resolves the question: Come now! Receive!

2. *Jesus wants to do miracles through you.* "Anyone believing in Me shall do the same miracles I have done, and even greater ones, because I am going to be with the Father" (John 14:12). Miracles do not require that you become strange, nor are they a substitute for maturing in Christ. But when the Holy Spirit fills you, He makes miracles timely and normal—given in God's timing and ministered in His spirit of love.

3. *This is the gateway to the gifts of the Spirit.* "He will take of what is Mine and declare it to you" (John 16:14, NKJV). Among the many things He did, Jesus was notably involved in healing and delivering people as He spoke with loving and holy grace and power. Today, the gifts of the Spirit are the means by which the Holy Spirit advances that work of Christ. He distributes those same workings of Jesus to and through the members of Christ's Body—His Church (See 1 Corinthians 12:7-13.).

HOW TO RECEIVE THE FULLNESS OF THE HOLY SPIRIT

Everyone who thirsts for Christ's deeper, fuller work in their lives asks how it can be done. My personal feeling is that to tell someone "exactly how" to be filled is to risk substituting a man-devised formula for what Jesus wants to do Himself. He is both ready and able to satisfy your quest without help from anyone else. So in the light of all I've said, my simple encouragement to you now is: "Go directly to Him. Bow before Him. Open to Him. Trust Him—and ask Jesus to fill you with His Holy Spirit."

There are several thoughts—words I have often used to help any who feels hesitant, fearful, or in need of further instruction. But, before I share those, could I first just invite you to *pray?* Your own words are sufficient. But if you believe the prayer I offer here will help you, then make it your own. No matter now you pray, the way to be filled now is to come, thirsty and believing—for the thirsty *will* be filled, and the promise *is yours* (See Acts 2:39; Matthew 5:6.)

Come to Jesus—for He's the Baptizer, and He *wants* to fill you. (See John 1:33.).

Dear Lord Jesus,

I thank You and praise You for Your great love and faithfulness to me. My heart is filled with joy whenever I think of the great gift of salvation You have so freely given to me, and I humbly glorify You, Lord Jesus; for You have forgiven me all my sins and brought me to the Father.

Now I come in obedience to Your call. I want to receive the fullness of the Holy Spirit. I do not come because I am worthy myself, but because

You have invited me to come.

Because You have washed me from my sins, I thank You that You have made the vessel of my life a worthy one to be filled with the Holy Spirit of God. I want to be overflowed with Your life, Your love, and Your power, Lord Jesus. I want to show forth Your grace, Your words, Your goodness, and Your gifts to everyone I can.

And so, with simple, childlike faith, I ask You, Lord: Fill me with the Holy Spirit. I open all of myself to You to receive all of Yourself in me. I love You, Lord, and I lift my voice in praise to You. I welcome Your might and Your miracles. May they be made manifest in me—for Your glory and for Your praise.

I don't tell people to say "Amen" at the end of this prayer because, after inviting Jesus to fill you, it is good to begin to praise Him in faith. Praise and worship Jesus, and simply allow the Holy Spirit to help you do so. He will manifest Himself in a Christ-glorifying way, and you can ask Him to enrich this moment by causing you to know the presence and power of the Lord Jesus. Don't hesitate to expect the same things in your experience as occurred to people in the Bible. The spirit of praise is an appropriate way to express that expectation and to make Jesus your focus by worshiping as you praise. Glorify Him and leave the rest to the Holy Spirit.

STEPPING INTO A MIRACLE

Through years of ministry, I have found that Peter's experience of walking on the water is a striking parallel to the step of faith being taken by believers who want to enter the walk of the Spirit-filled. Here is the account from Matthew 14:22-33:

> "Immediately after this, Jesus told His disciples to get into their boat and cross over to the other side of the lake while He stayed to get the people started home. Then afterwards He went up into the hills to pray. Night fell, and out on the lake the disciples were in trouble for the wind had risen and they were fighting heavy seas. About four o'clock in the morning Jesus came to them, walking on the water! They screamed in terror, for they thought He was a ghost. But Jesus immediately spoke to them, reassuring them. 'Don't be afraid!' He said.
>
> "Then Peter called to Him: 'Sir, if it is really You, tell me to come over to You, walking on the water.' 'All right,' the Lord said, 'come along!' So Peter went over the side of the boat and walked on the water toward Jesus. But when he looked around at the high waves, he was terrified and began to sink. 'Save me, Lord!' he shouted. Instantly Jesus reached

out His hand and rescued him. 'O man
of little faith,' Jesus said. 'Why did you
doubt Me?' And when they had climbed
back into the boat, the wind stopped.
The others sat there, awestruck. 'You really are the Son of God!' they exclaimed."

Receiving the fullness of the Holy Spirit is
very much the same as answering a call to walk
on the water, for it is a call to begin walking
in the arena of the miraculous. I emphasize this
miraculous dimension of life not because I believe
we should seek the miraculous for the sake of
sensation, but because we should expect the
Spirit-filled life to have the same qualities that
characterized the early Church's experience of
Spirit-fullness.

When believers received the Holy Spirit on
the occasions the Bible describes, special things
always happened: people lifted their voices in
praise (worship); people spoke forth God's Word
(prophecy); evidence of God's presence was
unusually seen (signs); miracles took place
(wonders).

It is understandable that some people fear
being thought fanatical for expecting such biblical
manifestations. Enough isolated episodes of folly
have taken place to provide stimulus to those
fears. But it is also understandable why many are
not only unafraid but boldly expectant that such
present-day evidence of the Holy Spirit's fullness
will occur. After all, if the One who distributes

the gifts (the Holy Spirit Himself) is the One the Lord Jesus is pouring in fullness over the life of the prayerful, praising believer, then it is altogether reasonable to expect signs of His presence and willingness to give!

As you come to be filled, consider the following steps:

STEP ONE: *"Cross to the Other Side"* (v.22)

Peter's "miracle day" began by simply obeying Jesus' command to get in the ship and head out across the lake.

The beginning for any of us seeking to be filled with the Spirit today—this very day—is to obey the Lord Jesus. Be certain that no known disobedience is being secretly sheltered from His open gaze and dealing.

For example: Have you been baptized in water? Have you confessed any reserved, secret sin? Are there any people you need to forgive? Are there any amends for past sins that you can and should make? Is there any condemnation you carry that needs to be laid to rest under the blood of Jesus?

You may not be able to take care of all of these matters in one day, but you can make a commitment before the Lord Jesus now to surrender these things to Him and be open to His leading in the future. Then proceed expectantly, moving "toward the other side" in obedience.

STEP TWO: *"Be of Good Cheer! It Is I"*
(v.27, NKJV)

The tossing waves and the Man walking toward the boat over those stormy waves presented Peter with a frightening setting. In his uncertainty, he even mistook the Lord he knew so well for a ghost (v. 25,26). But with Jesus' words of comfort, "It is I," the complexion of everything changed. When Peter was sure it was Jesus approaching and not some spirit, he was prepared for the miracle that followed.

Similarly, there are stormy waters of fear stirred up by some people today on the subject of Spirit-fullness. As with Peter, they can often distract us from seeing that in the midst of it all *Jesus* is coming to invite us to walk with Him in a miracle. Once the understanding is settled that "This is all about Him, and His will for me," the peace of God makes room for receptive faith to operate simply and fulfillingly.

STEP THREE: *"If it is really You, tell me to come"* (v.28)

Peter's confidence to answer Jesus' invitation to come, to walk with Him in a miracle, was established on the grounds that he *knew* Him. When Jesus said, "Come," the responding action was born of a *relationship*, not a foolish presumption.

The same is true today with you and me. The desire of walking with Jesus Christ in a "miracle

walk" may sound to some as though we seek
that walk for self glorifying or sensational reasons.
But our freedom to expect a new "miracle work"
and respond accordingly is rooted in the understanding that Jesus is both the Giver and the
Goal of that walk. Our focus is on *Him*, and we
seek to see all glory given to *Him*. Seeking to
receive the fullness of the Holy Spirit is *not* a
quest for selfish gratification; it is a desire to
walk with Christ at a dimension of life to which
He calls us. No less!

STEP FOUR: *"All right," the Lord said, "Come along"* (v.29)

Peter walked on the water! It's startling enough
that Jesus did that, but for an ordinary human
being to do the same is overwhelming. We don't
overlook that. Peter later feared, doubted, and
sank. But even this carries a doubly marvelous
fact: he was rescued and restored! Peter walked
on the water twice!

I know of no passage of Scripture that more
closely parallels the desire of the Lord Jesus Christ
to welcome us into full partnership with His
power and purpose. He invites us to "Come!"

So, do that!

Come and receive the fullness of the Holy
Spirit and let Him usher you into a miracle walk
at a new dimension of prayer, power, and living.
This experience will not guarantee your perfection any more than it did Peter's. But in the same

way that Peter survived by calling upon the Lord, you can count on Jesus to keep you safe. He'll sustain you in your new walk with Him as you receive the Holy Spirit in fullness.

Come and walk with Jesus in a miracle!

CHAPTER SIX

The Pathway in The Promise

RECEIVING THE FULLNESS of the Holy Spirit is not a climax—it is a commencement. The Bible record makes that point from the beginning: "Everyone present was filled with the Holy Spirit and began...." (Acts 2:4). From that start those early believers experienced a broad development of "beginnings," from miraculously enabled praise to their endurance of fierce persecution and martyrdom.

If the Bible teaches us anything about this miracle dimension of life in the Spirit, it shows it to be a dimension of adventure and adversity. Because it is a qualifying experience for moving into arenas of spiritual conquest, we can be sure there will be both joyous blessing and distinct seasons of struggle, confrontation with evil, and spiritual warfare. There is no such thing as victory without battle.

But the prospect of facing this facet of Holy Spirit-fullness should discourage no one for three reasons. First, you are equipped for triumph—although the battle may be heated at points, victory is certain in Christ. Second, battles are not continuous—there are seasons of reprieve, rest, and joy untainted by present conflicts. Third,

Jesus walked this way before you—He has blazed the trail ahead and marked out the dangers, and, by His guidance, you can avoid the pitfalls and walk with confidence.

Once you are Spirit-filled, you will want to take a very close look at what is coming. We are given a pathway of practical follow-through in the account of Jesus' experience after He was filled with the Spirit:

"Then Jesus was led out into the wilderness by the Holy Spirit, to be tempted there by Satan. For forty days and forty nights He ate nothing and became very hungry.

Then Satan tempted Him to get food by changing stones into loaves of bread. 'It will prove You are the Son of God,' he said.

"But Jesus told him, 'No! For the Scriptures tell us that bread won't feed men's souls: obedience to every word of God is what we need.'

"Then Satan took Him to Jerusalem to the roof of the Temple. 'Jump off,' he said, and prove You are the Son of God; for the Scriptures declare 'God will send His angels to keep You from harm...they will prevent You from smashing on the rocks below.'

"Jesus retorted, 'It also says not to put the Lord your God to a foolish test!'

"Next Satan took Him to the peak of a very high mountain and showed Him the nations of the world and all their glory. 'I'll give it all to you,' he said, 'if You will only kneel and worship me.'

"'Get out of here, Satan,' Jesus told him. 'The Scriptures say, "Worship only the Lord God. Obey only Him.'

"Then Satan went away and angels came and cared for Jesus" (Matthew 4:1-11).

This passage gives five clear guidelines concerning a person's walk in the new dimension of Spirit-fullness. By seeing what happened to Jesus in the days immediately following the Holy Spirit's coming upon Him for ministry, we can learn these five truths:

ONE: *Don't be surprised if the adversary attacks you right away*

There are many people who suppose that being "led of the Spirit" means you will never experience trials. Beware of such euphoric notions! The experience of the Lord Jesus was one of immediate conflict with the Devil, and it is very clear that it was the Holy Spirit who led Him into that confrontation. Do you think your experience will be any different?

To the contrary, Peter says, "Dear friends, don't be bewildered or surprised when you go through the fiery trials ahead, for this is no strange, unusual thing that is going to happen to you...Be careful—watch out for attacks from Satan, your great enemy. He prowls around like a hungry, roaring lion looking for some victim to tear apart" (1 Peter 4:12; 5:8).

Moving into the Spirit-filled life is moving into confrontation with the enemy. But don't hesitate and never fear; for "You are of God, little children, and have overcome them, because He who is in you is greater than he who is in the world" (1 John 4:4, NKJV).

Every step of spiritual advance is countered by an attempt of Satan to check that forward movement. Doubt is a common weapon. For example, when you first received Christ, didn't you find the Adversary trying to make you doubt the reality of your salvation? Or, when you've taken a step of faith, have you ever been tormented by the question, "Can I be sure God's Word is reliable?" And among the most common experiences of believers who have been recently filled with the Spirit is Satan's accusation: "Who do you think you are? You haven't *really* been filled!" Then he will cite your weaknesses—a logical tactic designed to take your attention away from your new resource of strength. If he can get you to wonder about the reality of what you have received, he can force you on the defensive just at the time Christ wants to prepare you for attack.

This strategic device of the Devil is notably present in his conversation with Jesus. When he says, "It will prove You are the Son of God" (Matthew 4:3), the Adversary is approaching Jesus with a defiance intended to intimidate. It's as though he is saying, "Since You're supposed to be someone so special…" or, "Who do You think You are?" He uses the same ruse on us, and often we back down too easily, whispering inwardly, "Perhaps I'm not as specifically prepared as I thought."

But Jesus' bold responses call us to equal boldness. When the Enemy challenges your authority in Christ, you may freely reply: "I am special. I am a redeemed child of the Most High God. Furthermore, I resist all fear and doubt in the Name of my Lord—Jesus Christ. He's more special than anyone, anytime, and anywhere, and I am complete in Him."

TWO: *Beware of any inclination to be self-serving*

In light of the fact that Jesus was just concluding His forty-day fast, the Devil's suggestion that Jesus turn the stones to bread was a very practical temptation. There would have been nothing improper about Christ eating bread, and on the face of it there was no reason to deny His right to work a miracle. But Jesus rejects the Devil's proposition and, in doing so, provides us with this insight: We may be tempted to use the powerful resources of Spirit-filled living for selfish reasons unless we keep them under God's rulership.

Perhaps the earliest temptation that newly Spirit-filled believers face is the desire to flaunt their experience. There are so many ways this can be done, even with acceptable social grace. But at the heart, the honest believer knows when he is trying to "slip something in," to use his spiritual experience as a credential of some supposed status of maturity or superiority. The primary and ultimate evidence of the Holy Spirit in anyone's life is love, and love will never seek its own advantage or do anything to inflate its own importance (See 1 Corinthians 13:4,5.)

THREE: *If the power of the Holy Spirit is in your life, you don't have to prove it.*

The crafty serpent worms his way into a position of making his suggestions appear spiritual. Notice how the Devil quotes Scripture to Jesus (Matthew 4:6). Of course, Jesus knows the Liar for what he is; He knows Satan will never seek to motivate you toward a good work or toward a point of obeying God's Word or will. When Satan dared Jesus to leap from the high place, the last thing he wanted to do was demonstrate the power of God. So you can be certain that any presumptuous suggestion he makes to you is another effort to deceive.

A normal response to having received the fullness of the Holy Spirit is to gain a deeper compassion for the lost, a greater readiness to serve, or a more heightened hunger for spiritual pursuit. Unfortunately, some who have not been taught the Adversary's devices have succumbed to his deceptions. Upon their introduction to Spirit-filled living, they soon try to put out an exaggerated or imbalanced effort at godliness. It is not uncommon to see them neglect good sense and practical duty in the name of being "more spiritual." Worse yet, they are misled by the Devil into trying to prove their spiritual superiority at the expense of others who should be more sensitively and sensibly served.

For example, one young man was so excited about his newly discovered dimension of power, insight, and equipping through the Holy Spirit that he suddenly left his job, uprooted his family, and thrust himself out as an evangelist seeking public meetings. There's no question that he had been given a gift for such a ministry, but his timing and approach to that ministry were miles off the mark. He ended up with a disillusioned wife, frustrated kids, and considerable debt; and with it all he wondered why God had let him down. Of course, the failure wasn't God's. The failure was the man's for giving in to the ploy of the Adversary, as he prodded, "Go on, show your stuff, how that you're mighty in God."

You never need to prove the power of God in your life. The Lord may call you to steps of faith, but He never calls to flights of fancy. And if you ever need to test what you may be feeling or hearing, seek out mature, faith-filled spiritual leaders with sufficient depth and boldness of belief to hear your heart and counsel you.

FOUR: *You will find new opportunities to declare the Lordship of Christ in your life*

Jesus was pointedly challenged by Satan to bow to him, and we wonder that such a suggestion was even made. Did Satan really think for one moment that God's Son would consider the proposal—even using all the world's wealth and power as the lure? Whatever the answer may be, Jesus' outright and complete refusal of Satan's detestable proposition shows this lovely fact: that hellish summons only gave Jesus one more opportunity to affirm His full-hearted allegiance to the Father. His answer was, "Get out of here, Satan! The scriptures say 'Worship only the Lord God. Obey only Him'"(v.10). This provides us with a healthy reminder: The flesh—though Spirit-filled and holy—still depends on humility in worship and service before God to sustain its life in Him.

With respect to all that takes place when we are filled with the Spirit, one thing to keep in mind is this: You are no less "flesh" for having been Spirit-filled. Paul's letter to the Galatians takes up that theme: "Having begun in the Spirit, do you think you can become complete and mature through the energy of the flesh?" (Galatians 3:3, author's paraphrase). To the Romans he cautioned, "If you live according to the flesh you will die; but if by the Spirit you put to death the deeds of the body, you will live" (Romans 8:13, NKJV). Both of these words of counsel were directed to people who understood what being Spirit-filled meant. And these words clearly warn us that, with all the joy, the power, the love, and the thrill—none of these features of fullness preempts a continual monitoring of the flesh. The flesh will always seek its own way, and though the vessel is Spirit-filled, it is, nonetheless, still flesh.

This doesn't mean the presence of the Holy Spirit makes no difference at all, for His infilling makes a very real difference. The point is that the fullness of the Spirit will bring additional opportunities for you to newly and freshly declare the Lordship of Jesus in your life. And with that confrontation, our selfishness, pride, or carnality will be faced. Just remember, when you do face these things, the power you have been given is only for serving God—not yourself.

FIVE: *Keeping full of God's Word is the best way to keep filled with God's Spirit*

The recurrence in this text of these words falling from Jesus' lips, "The Scriptures say…The Scriptures say…," is an inescapable commentary on the pathway of Spirit-filled living. Jesus meets each situation with the Word of God. When we do the same, the Word becomes a flashing sword in the grip of a warrior, slicing through the froth of superficiality, cutting through the flesh of carnality, and striking down the Adversary.

Such an immediate availability of the Word

when battle strikes or when temptation flares is not the result of casual reading. Feeding upon the Word with regular habit, as certainly as one usually keeps regular mealtimes, is not only a powerful practice but is specifically taught in the midst of Jesus' test: "Bread won't feed men's souls; obedience to every word of God is what we need" (Matthew 4:4).

The essential point to understand is that we are not dealing with a generalized or academic approach to the Bible. *Hearing* and *studying* the Word of God are both very desirable practices, and both are taught in the Scriptures. But hearing without *doing* and studying without *applying* are dangerous to even the most sincere among us (See James 1:22.). What keeps the Word of God at hand—ready for confrontation with flesh or devil—is allowing the Holy Spirit to infuse it into your spiritual system. Spirit-filled living calls for hearing, studying, doing, and applying the Word, for then all become joyfully dynamic with the Spirit's aid.

There's nothing more fulfilling, nor more certain to integrate the spirit of the Word into the substance of your living, than bringing the Word to life through obedience to these words: "Let the word of Christ dwell in you richly in all wisdom, teaching and admonishing one another in psalms and hymns and spiritual songs, singing with grace in your hearts to the Lord" (Colossians 3:16, NKJV).

The pathway of promised life in the Spirit is

one that invites us to learn to walk in God's wisdom and by God's power. Periodic warfare gains accumulated victories, while interim seasons of rejoicing are preparatory for our next conflict and conquest. It's an unlimited journey into joy, with a ceaseless promise of hope.

> "But the good man walks along in the ever-brightening light of God's favor; the day gives way to morning splendor" (Proverbs 4:18).

CHAPTER SEVEN

The Panorama of The Promise

There is always the danger that, in describing our human experience of God's working in our lives, we will, however unintentionally, reduce our view of God to a humanistic level—taking "God down to our size," so to speak. Of course, God is not offended at our need to understand Him in human terms, for that is the very reason He became flesh. In the person of Jesus, He became touchable by and understandable to all mankind.

Yet when we speak of the limited and finite frame of one human being receiving "the fullness of the Holy Spirit," we are attempting to express something that can't actually be described with precision. The words we use are scriptural, but the concept is spiritual and it's good to understand its meaning.

To begin, being "filled" with God certainly does not mean that "all there is of God" has been fit into a human being. What it does mean is that the essence of His nature, the resource of His power, and the presence of His person have come to abide within us in a real and personal way.

Just as a child's bucket may be filled with water from the ocean as he stands on the shore without diminishing the enormity of the sea, so

God's greatness is not diminished by giving of Himself to be poured into us.

When we receive of His fullness, the Holy Spirit comes in as an earnest of our inheritance, a down payment, or a guarantee of more to come, a small taste of all that is in store (See Ephesians 1:14.). Beyond that, the Bible says infinite abundance awaits us in the future, for "in the ages to come He might show the exceeding riches of His grace...in Christ Jesus" (Ephesians 2:7 NKJV).

The prospect of having an eternity to grow in our understanding of God's goodness is a part of our inheritance in Christ. And yet a very present feature of His grace is that He has *now* opened to us a constantly expanding resource of His life and fullness. This is especially true since you have opened to the full working of His Holy Spirit and He has come in power to expand and expedite that life-flow from Christ.

The unfolding panorama of promise before each newly Spirit-filled believer opens his opportunity to move into the deepened experience of the fruit of the Holy Spirit, and into the dynamic exercise of His gifts. Entire books are written on the subject of the Holy Spirit's fruit and gifts, so I'll include just an introductory overview of these provisions of God, listing the foundational texts concerning the fruit and the gifts, and setting them side by side for comparison.

Because the fruit of the Spirit involve character, as compared with the gifts (which involve divinely-given abilities), some people tend to prioritize or neglect one at the expense of the other.

For example, some will say, "*How* you live for Christ is more important than *what* you do for Him. So the fruit is more important." While another will say, "There is so great a need for powerful help to meet human need, let's get on with gifts; fruit can grow later." But we should note that God's Word does not prioritize one above the other. Even the fact that they number the same—nine each—seems to be a pointer toward God's heavenly balance on the issue.

We can be used in the gifts while we grow in the fruit of the Spirit. All of these processes are for us *now.* They are all of grace and they are all for Jesus Christ's glory. Open yourself to both—fully and completely. Learn what you can and move ahead in a Spirit-filled life to fruitfulness and ministry.

Perhaps the most important thing we might learn about all these attributes and abilities is that none of them are permanent in the sense that they become automatic.

For example, the fruit of love can easily rot on the vine of a person's life if it is not nourished by today's fresh filling of the Spirit. Furthermore, no gift of the Spirit is intended to become your private possession. Each one is given for ministering—to give away, not to keep. So today's operation in the gifts of the Spirit doesn't qualify me for the same thing tomorrow—unless I keep freshly filled with the Spirit.

THE FRUIT OF THE SPIRIT

Text: Galatians 5:22, 23

"But when the Holy Spirit controls our lives,
He will produce this kind of fruit in us:
Love, joy, peace, patience, kindness, goodness,
faithfulness, gentleness and self-control."

Text: Ephesians 5:8-10 NKJV
"For you were once darkness, but now you are
light in the Lord. Walk as children of light
(for the fruit of the Spirit is in all goodness,
righteousness and truth), proving what is
acceptable to the Lord."

FRUIT

Love
Joy
Peace
Patience
Kindness
Goodness
Faithfulness
Gentleness
Self-control

PURPOSE

The fruit of the Spirit focus on the person of
Christ being manifest in our life for Him.

THE GIFTS OF THE SPIRIT

Text: 1 Corinthians 121:7-11, NKJV

"But the manifestation of the Spirit is given to each one for the profit of all: for to one is given the word of wisdom through the Spirit, to another the word of knowledge through the same Spirit, to another faith by the same Spirit, to another gifts of healings by the same Spirit, to another the working of miracles, to another prophecy, to another discerning of spirits, to another different kinds of tongues, to another the interpretation of tongues."

GIFTS

A word of wisdom
A word of knowledge
Faith
Healings
Working of miracles
Prophecy
Discerning of spirits
Tongues
Interpretation of tongues

PURPOSE

The gifts of the Spirit focus on the power of Christ being manifest through our life for Him.

KEEPING FULL OF THE HOLY SPIRIT

A comparative study of the life, ministry, and prayer of the early Church in the Book of Acts shows that those who were filled with the Spirit at Pentecost had recurrent "fillings" with the Spirit on later occasions (See Acts 2:4; 4:8; 4:31; and compare 9:17 with 13:9.). This is not a commentary on the Holy Spirit's lack of commitment to us; He does not move in and out of those He indwells or fills. Rather, when He comes, He comes to abide and remain with us: "But the anointing which you have received from Him abides in you" (1 John 2:27, NJKV).

And yet we each hold a very real human capacity to lose our sense of His presence or to somehow grieve the Spirit through insensitivity or disobedience. There also is a tremendous "drain off" that occurs through the daily business of performing our personal duties or pursuing our spiritual service for Christ. The reservoir of heaven is abundantly adequate and always full, but the channel of our souls seems limited to receiving just today's supply. Paul spoke of this, describing to the Philippians his ability to survive the rigors of imprisonment only as he received the supply of the Spirit of Christ (See Philippians 1:19.).

So in this light it is understandable that we are called to learn a daily walk of dependency and a regular pattern of *re*-filling. The Ephesians were commanded, "Be filled...with the Holy Spirit" (Ephesians 5:18), and the present imperative form of the verb makes the literal command read, "Be continually being filled!" With that command, another aspect of the promised life in the Spirit unfolds: The call to be filled is a summons to experience the ongoing beauty and endless glory that awaits those who will keep coming back for more.

There is a pattern of life that will ensure continual fullness of the Spirit, and it is maintained through three basics: (1) worship and praise, (2) feeding on the Word, and (3) faithful obedience. Take these three rules of life and apply them, and there is no reason you ever need to be less than "full of faith and of the Holy Spirit," as was Stephen (Acts 6:5).

1. WORSHIP AND PRAISE

The previously quoted command of Ephesians 5 gives a simple directive to sing much: "quoting psalms and hymns and singing sacred songs, making music in your hearts to the Lord" (v.19). It is not only refreshing to enter the Lord's presence with daily worship but also refilling. Song-filled, private, Holy Spirit-enabled praise is a key to keeping renewed—freshly filled with the Spirit.

2. FEEDING ON THE WORD

In Peter's second letter, he writes of the Lord: "His divine power has given to us all things that pertain to life and godliness, through the knowledge of Him who called us by glory and virtue, by which have been given to us exceedingly great and precious promises, that through these you may be partakers of the divine nature" (2 Peter 1:3,4, NKJV).

The distilled truth of these words is this: The precious promises of God's holy Word are a resource for keeping full of His holy nature. His power has given us what we need; now we need only to be partakers of that ongoing grace by receiving regular input through the Word.

3. FAITHFUL OBEDIENCE

It is impossible to keep filled with the Holy Spirit while walking in willful disobedience. The biblical commands not to "grieve the Holy Spirit" (Ephesians 4:30) or "quench the Spirit" (1 Thessalonians 5:19) both emphasize this fact. When the Holy Spirit is grieved, He will let you know it. He will not abandon you; He will signal you concerning any action, thought, or attitude that displeases Him.

Confession and obedience result in His continued presence. But indifference or rebellion can quench Him, that is, drown out His voice or suffocate the flame of His power.

Stay sensitively obedient…and obediently sensitive. The reward of ongoing fullness with His abiding presence and power is well worth it.

An increase of the Holy Spirit's power is the ongoing potential for all who open their hearts to His fullness and who will continue to learn the life of Spirit-filled possibilities. Just as you first come to Jesus to be filled, you must walk with

Jesus and stay filled. The surgings of the Holy Spirit will sweep over you daily and keep you ever-prepared for Christ's highest purpose for all of your life and in all of His will.

> "All my days I want to live here
>   At the fountainhead of life
> Always drinking in the fullness
>   Of the Spirit of Jesus Christ.
> All my being in submission
>   To His Word and to His will
> All my spirit opened heavenward
>   That His love my vessel fill.
> Spirit-filled I ask to be, Lord
>   Spirit-filled I want to stay,
> Ever, always, constant, steady,
>   Filled with power and filled
>   with praise.

CHAPTER EIGHT

Questions About Being Spirit-Filled

In my years of pastoral ministry, I have encountered common questions related to being Spirit-filled. This brief series of questions and answers is provided for your study and help.

What is the sin against the Holy Spirit?

There is a remarkable recurrence of this question on "the unpardonable sin," or "the sin against the Holy Spirit." It is certainly understandable since any sin that had no point of forgiveness with God would be the first one any thoughtful person would want to know of and avoid.

The grounds for this question are in the Word, because Jesus Himself spoke of a sin for which there is no forgiveness. The Scripture reads:

> "Even blasphemy against Me or any other sin can be forgiven—all except one: speaking against the Holy Spirit shall never be forgiven, either in this world or in the world to come" (Matthew 12:31, 32, [See also Mark 3:28-30 and Luke 12:10.]).

Two definitions are given of this sin. First, the most obvious is any word a person would speak that was forthrightly blasphemous against the Holy Spirit—the Third Person of the Trinity. Exactly how someone might do that is subject to interpretation; consequently, a widely diverse description of that action exists among believers.

However, Jesus seems to make it clear in the context of the passages that the essence of this sin lies in attributing the work of the Holy Spirit to Satan (Mark 3:30). For example, recently there have been some who have attributed the exercise of some spiritual gifts to demons, and others have been quick to say those making such an accusation have committed this unpardonable sin.

That seems doubtful, however, for it appears that the situation Jesus addressed involved something deeper than theological misunderstanding. In the text, the heart of the matter was human resistance against God's present work, resistance to the point that hardened hearts insisted on their own righteousness as opposed to God's working. The Pharisees virtually made themselves God by attributing Jesus' doings to the Devil.

In other words, they determined that the Holy Spirit at work through Jesus was so offensive to them that they made a judgment against Him and took the same position as Lucifer: "I will be like the Most High God" (Isaiah 14:12-15). For this—establishing one's own rightness in opposition to God's—there is no forgiveness. God Himself has thereby been removed or overruled by the individual's own order of things; therefore, eternal loss is the only option remaining. This conclusion has led some to take an alternate position concerning the definition of this sin.

Some see the unpardonable sin as the individual's rejection of Jesus Christ as God's Messiah, the Savior of the world. Since the ministry of the Holy Spirit is to testify to Jesus' Saviorhood and mankind's need of Him (See John 16:8-11.). It is argued that the willful rejection of the Holy Spirit's efforts to bringing you to Christ is the sin against the Holy Spirit. Therefore, of course, no salvation—and no forgiveness is available (See John 14:6; Acts 4:12.).

In any case, regardless of the precise definition, the sin against the Holy Spirit is not a matter that needs to preoccupy any sincere believer. Experience has taught me that there are inevitably a certain number of earnest, seeking, semi-informed souls who will become trapped by the fear that they have committed this sin. Lying spirits and human guilt combine to reinforce this misconception.

Whenever I am confronted by such a person, who—whether weeping or stolidly passive because they are convinced they are guilty of this unforgivable sin—I offer this answer: If you are concerned as to whether you have committed the unpardonable sin, you haven't. The very fact that you care and that you hope you haven't committed it is evidence in itself that the Holy Spirit is still dealing with your heart and He is ready to bring you into peace and forgiveness—which are both fully available to you.

If the lie persists, by whatever voice—internal mocking or condemning fear—speak against it in the Name of Jesus Christ of Nazareth. Through the blood of His cross, declare your full acceptance of His saving, atoning death and resurrection life as your grounds for salvation and acceptance by the heavenly Father. Don't let Satan have a field day by distorting a truth that has nothing whatsoever to do with you. He—the Devil—has committed this sin, and it is not surprising that he tries to spread his hopeless despair to others. Instead, if you or anyone you counsel is tormented by his ensnaring device, resist the Devil and order him to flee from you. Stand in the liberty of the Lord Jesus Christ and rejoice in the blessings of His mercy, His forgiveness, and His abiding love (Galatians 5:1; 1 Peter 1:6-9; 5:8,9).

How holy must a person be to qualify for the fullness of the Spirit?

Acts 2:38, 39 makes clear that being filled with the Holy Spirit is a *gift*. It also establishes that it is a *promised* gift to anyone who comes to Christ in repentance and who follows Christ in water baptism. This promise is offered on the same terms as salvation. Beyond that, there is no preliminary qualification, special merit or holiness required to receive the fullness of the Spirit.

In this respect, it may be helpful to take

special notice of the difference between "the *gift* of the Holy Spirit" (Acts 2:38) and "the *gifts* of the Holy Spirit" (1 Corinthians 12:7-11). The *gift* (singular) is the Holy Spirit Himself, given by the Father (Luke 11:13) to all who obey Him (Acts 5:32), and poured forth by the hand of Jesus, His Son (John 1:33; Acts 2:33).

The only primary qualifying factor that Christ reveals for receiving the fullness of God is a genuine hunger and thirst for His righteousness—for the pure power of His working (Matthew 5:6).

May a person be filled with the Holy Spirit without being baptized in water?

The overwhelming work of the Spirit that took place when Peter preached to the household of Cornelius (Acts 10:24-48) makes it clear that water baptism is not a legal requirement for receiving the fullness of the Holy Spirit. But at the same time, the immediacy with which Peter instructed those who had just been filled to be baptized in water at once, indicates the importance of *both* in the divine order of things.

The notion that "Holy Spirit baptism" (or any other spiritual experience) might remove the need for water baptism is a deception. It suggests a status system that puts higher value on one point of obedience than another. We are taught to do both: (1) be baptized in water (Acts 2:38) and (2) be baptized with the Holy Spirit (Acts 1:5; John 1:33).

What is the difference between "the baptism with the Holy Spirit," "being filled with the Holy Spirit," and "becoming Spirit-filled"?

These are generally interchangeable terms, and the fact that a variety of phrases is used for the same spiritual experience shouldn't bother us. A rigid, legal insistence of terms may become "religiously" correct, but the experience is more important than the set of words used to describe it.

For example, when someone "receives Christ as Savior," that experience is also frequently described as "being saved," "being born again," or "being converted."

It is possible to use *both* biblical phraseology and descriptive phraseology. Perhaps we would usually prefer the biblical terms, but there is nothing in the Bible that disallows the use of our own words in describing our experience. The only rule should be that we always go back to the Bible as the *standard* of our experience, never letting either human terms or human experience become the standard by themselves. To do so is to eventually fall into humanistic practices without scriptural basis and eventually to fall into confusion and error.

Doesn't the Bible say that every believer is "baptized by one spirit into one body," and thereby every believer should be said to have already been baptized with the Holy Spirit when they are saved, when they received Christ?

This perfectly understandable question, based on 1 Corinthians 12:13, is often raised by people who object to being invited as believers in Christ to receive the baptism with the Holy Spirit. While I do not use the same terminology, I generally accept their preference that the term *Holy Spirit baptism* be reserved for their new birth.

Nonetheless, there is ample evidence in the Word that this term is used for the occasion at which a person is *filled* with the Holy Spirit. John 1:33 relates this ministry of "baptizer with the Holy Spirit" as a distinct work of Christ in His ministry as "Lamb of God who takes away the world's sin" (John 1:29, 33). Further, Jesus Himself urged His disciples to remain in Jerusalem, for "you shall be baptized with the Holy Spirit in just a few days" (Acts 1:5). Many feel that these texts indicate a difference between the baptism *by* the Holy Spirit and the baptism *in* the Spirit. The first is the Holy Spirit's baptism as He brings the repentant believer unto and into Christ. The second is Jesus' baptism as He fills and overflows His own with the power of the Holy Spirit.

It is probably best not to belabor this to the point of division in the Church. The actual Greek preposition used in both texts is the same (*en*), and can be translated either as "in," "with," or "by," depending upon the translator's understanding of the text.

Regardless of differences in terminology, however, the one inescapable fact is that the Word calls us to *both*—repentance and baptism in water (enter *into* Christ) *and* Holy Spirit fullness (given us *by* Christ). To fail to seek the fullness of the Holy Spirit because of a supposition that salvation already accomplishes that is to either misunderstand or misconstrue Scripture.

What place do "tongues" have in the work of the Holy Spirit?

The spectrum of opinion on "tongues" runs all the way from sturdy opposition to an insistence that it is the first physical sign of a person's becoming Spirit-filled. This is unfortunate when we consider (1) the place that God gave this sign, (2) the statement Jesus made about it, and (3) the observations Paul boldly declares.

First, the fact that the Church was born at Pentecost with this sign upon its lips makes it impossible to consider it insignificant: "They were all filled with the Holy Spirit and began to speak with other tongues as the Spirit gave them utterance" (Acts 2:4). With His creative resources as God Almighty, He might have designed any one of ten thousand things as indicators or signals of His working on so historic an occasion as the beginning of the Church. As it is, He chose "speaking with tongues" as one phenomenon to be included, and considering its recurrence elsewhere in the early Church, it cannot be consigned to a "one-time-only" concept. God must see some importance in the practice;

otherwise He probably would not have started the Church with it.

Second, Jesus prophesied that those who believe in Him "shall speak with new tongues" (Mark 16:17). Were it not for the miracle nature of the sign as it occurs throughout the rest of the New Testament following this prophecy, we might have thought He was merely foretelling the fact that people of various nations would come to faith in Him. But the evidence of the Scriptures will not allow us to honestly accept the meaning of His forecast about "tongues" as only being native languages of believers in nations newly evangelized.

Third, quite remarkably, in spite of the fact that he had some difficulty with one congregation who ignorantly violated the proper use of "tongues," the Apostle Paul is still very bold to encourage the personal use of and expectancy toward the miracle of language in prayer and praise.

While on the one hand objecting to the Corinthians' indiscriminate public use of the capacity to speak with tongues (1 Corinthians 14:23), he freely expresses his regular use of spiritual language in private: "I thank God that I speak in tongues privately more than any of…you" (14:18). Paul unhesitatingly expresses his willingness to sing *both* with his understanding and with his spirit (14:15). Further, he affirms the validity of the exercise of tongues *if*—if it doesn't overshadow the exercise of gifts that serve the understanding (14:5).

When Paul concludes the 14th chapter of 1 Corinthians with a direct injunction to *not* prohibit the exercise of speaking with tongues (14:39) while requiring that public utterance must be disciplined and interpreted (14:27, 28), it seems that a vital, balanced teaching has been accomplished.

Is there a sign that a person has been filled with the Spirit?

The New Testament incidents where believers are specifically said to be filled with the Spirit help us answer this question. These narratives contain clear evidence of at least one fact: the fullness of the Holy Spirit will be shown in something holy and powerful. Study these cases:

1. At Pentecost the miracle of worshiping God in new languages occurred (Acts 2:1-13).
2. At Samaria, the text (Acts 8:9-24) clearly indicates that something remarkable enough to capture Simon's attention occurred. His quest to buy the power to confer the Holy Spirit upon people would not have taken place without the potential presence of some visible, physical manifestation. So such a carnal proposition could not have been prompted by a simple appreciation for some invisible, internalized experience that he'd been told of, but not seen.
3. In Acts 10:44, following Peter's ministry to Cornelius' household, the Holy Spirit "fell

upon them" and they spoke with tongues and prophesied. Both these actions are among the nine gifts of the Holy Spirit listed in 1 Corinthians 12. This clearly suggests that, at the very least, "gifts" of the Spirit might be expected to manifest when a believer receives the "gift" of the Spirit (Acts 2:39).

4. Paul's ministering the truth of the fullness of the Holy Spirit to the Ephesian disciples resulted in their speaking with tongues (Acts 19:1-6).

The significance of the four cases cited is that they are each *initiating* experiences; that is, those being filled with the Holy Spirit are experiencing their first taste of that fullness. This is not to be confused with the "refillings" that occur in such passages as Acts 4:8, 31, and 13:9, 52. Neither can we make a comparison with occasions of people being filled with the Spirit prior to Pentecost; such as Old Testament cases, or even New Testament examples such as Zacharias (Luke 1:67), Elizabeth (Luke 1:41), Mary (Luke 1:35) or John the Baptist (Luke 1:15).

That is a difficult question to answer only in the light of the arguments and misunderstandings that have plagued the Church on this subject. Sincere hearts do not want to violate the Holy Spirit of unity in the Body, yet honest minds cannot deny the evidence in the Word of God: Something supernatural ought to be expected when a person is initially filled with the Spirit.

To forge a formula and impose it on the Body is ultimately to reduce a precious, spontaneous experience to religious rigidity. But to remove the miracle dimension of expectancy from this experience is to reduce it to formalized tradition.

To my view, it is best that we open to Jesus Himself—He is the baptizer with the Holy Spirit (John 1:33). When love *for* Him becomes our motive and love *from* Him is poured upon us, there will be room for the Holy Spirit to work in fullness and in power. Let us hesitate to impose our doctrinal traditions or our dogmatic demands on those who honestly seek the Spirit's fullness. But let us not back away from any work of the Spirit that may humble our pride, cast out our fears, or melt our hearts.

What is "praying in the Spirit" or "praying with the Spirit"?

Examples of this are found in 1 Corinthians and Ephesians:

> "What is the result then? I will pray with the Spirit and I will also pray with the understanding. I will sing with the Spirit, and I will also sing with the understanding" (1 Corinthians 14:15, NKJV).

> "Praying always with all prayer and supplication in the Spirit, being watchful to this end with all perseverance and sup-

plication for all saints" (Ephesians 6:18, NKJV).

First, we should establish that all prayer uttered from the heart is heard by the Living God, no matter how weak or desperate the call (Psalm 86:7). Further, all prayer spoken in Jesus' Name is effective (John 14:13, 14; Acts 2:21). Certain prayers are not more worthy than others. God's heart is open to those who call upon Him, and He does not differentiate between "the spiritual prayers" and "the other ones."

But the multiplied dimensions of prayer are diverse, with a wide spectrum ranging from the basic request for daily bread to the bold attack of prayer in spiritual warfare. Devotional intimacy, praise-filled worship, contrite confession, joyous song, practical petition, insight-filled intercession, and spiritual conflict against demonic strongholds—all these are prayer forms, and the growing believer will grow in them.

There are times that the *intensity* of prayer (See Ephesians 6:10-18, "wrestling.") is such that a broadened dimension of prayer is needed. This may be manifest in *fervency* (James 5:16), i.e., "heated, impassioned prayer" offered in one's native tongue, or, as Paul said, he would pray on some occasions "with the Spirit." The fact that he is contrasting prayer "*with the Spirit*" with prayer "*with the understanding*," makes it clear in the context of the passage (1 Corinthians 15) that he is referring to the use of "tongues" at certain times in a person's private prayer life.

It would be incomplete to describe praying "with" or "in the Spirit" as *always* being "with tongues." But it would also be incomplete to describe it as *never* involving that exercise.

How may the gifts of the Holy Spirit be received and exercised?

Because the understanding of the Holy Spirit's gifts and their function is so broad a subject, this abbreviated answer is only intended to affirm that *you* are a candidate for these gifts. I can only encourage you to pursue them with an expectant heart.

The Bible says to "covet" spiritual gifts, i.e., "strongly desire" (1 Corinthians 14:1). That alone is evidence of God's desire that we move into the employment of these resources.

The key to all Holy Spirit operations is hunger and thirst, as Jesus said: "Blessed are those who hunger and thirst after righteousness, for they shall be filled." (Matthew 5:6, NKJV). This is not only a condition to being "filled"; it is the ongoing condition for living in His fullness.

The gifts of the Holy Spirit are fully available, and He is more than ready to distribute them *to* us and *through* us. "But one and the same Spirit works all these things, distributing to each one individually as He wills" (1 Corinthians 12:11 [See verses 1-11.]).

"As He wills" does not imply He is stingy,

grudgingly withholding gifts for the few who qualify. To the contrary, gifts of the Holy Spirit (Greek: *charismata*) are functions of God's grace (Greek: *charis*). The very inclusion of the word *grace* in this word for "gift" indicates the free availability of the Holy Spirit's operation and power to those who keep open to Him.

There is no status among the gifts. But, because the gifts are listed in a sequence, some people argue that some are more worthy than others. The fruit of the Spirit also are listed in an order, yet no one is foolish enough to suggest one characteristic to be more or less prized or significant than another. Also, you may occasionally hear someone suggest one gift is more desirable than another (example: wisdom), or to refer to "tongues" as the "least of the gifts." Of course, that isn't Scriptural. In fact, that quotation ("least of the gifts") is not in the Bible, but is of human invention.

The Holy Spirit makes the whole spectrum of gifts available to the believer who is wholeheartedly open. So the way you may receive the gifts of the Holy Spirit is to live in that openness and to exercise them in the spirit of His love.

Other Books by Jack Hayford

THE SPIRIT-FORMED LIFE

In a world with so much competing for our attention, it's easy to neglect or lose sight of the importance of the spiritual disciplines the Lord has given us for victorious living in Christ. Here is a path for new and matured believers alike, explaining the blessings of applying essential disciplines for personal and spiritual growth.

THE BEAUTY OF SPIRITUAL LANGUAGE

In a broad appeal that crosses denominational lines, Pastor Hayford makes a persuasive case for accepting tongues as a normal part of a Christian's experience. Anyone wanting an objective inquiry into the nature and biblical basis for this gift will appreciate *The Beauty of Spiritual Language*.

GROUNDS FOR LIVING

Grounds for Living is a great resource for every Christian. This teaching provides a rich exposition of God's Word, without losing sight of how doctrinal essentials may be applied to our lives daily, in a down-to-earth, practical way.

THE REWARD OF WORSHIP

Through this enriching study of God's Word on worship, you will learn to approach God's throne, the fountainhead of power, with praise that welcomes His creative touch. Worship unleashes a passion for both a global and very personal awakening as God is welcomed into our human circumstance.

Hope For A Hopeless Day

The words of Jesus, spoken from the Cross on what seemed to be His most hopeless day, hold keys that open doorways of hope for any hopeless day that we might face. While for Jesus, that Friday was a "bad" day, history calls it "Good" because of the unshakable hope His actions unleashed. As Jack Hayford discovered, in our darkest, most hopeless hour, Jesus declares, "Call on Me—I know the way through Fridays like yours, and I will bring you through!"

The Key To Everything

The Key To Everything unlocks the door to living in the spirit of God's releasing grace. Insights to our being released to give as you have received, forgive as you have been forgiving and serving as you have been gifted.

The Divine Visitor

Access growing in your understanding of God's love, as it is gloriously revealed in Christ's living among us, His being wounded and suffering for us, and His bleeding and dying for us.

For more resources, visit www.jackhayford.org

Additional copies of *Spirit-Filled* may be ordered through Foursquare Media in the online store at www.foursquaremedia.org or by phone at 1-800-992-7444 (option 1.)